Digital Dragon

The road to Nirvana runs through the Land of Tao

By Jan Krikke

Digital Dragon:
The road to Nirvana runs through the Land of Tao
Copyright © Jan Krikke, 2017
First Published 2017

Published by DCO Books, 2017
Bangkok Thailand
http://www.dco.co.th

ISBN 978-1981602148

Front cover credit: Jia Jia, Humanoid Robot. Photo courtesy of
University of Science and Technology of China in Hefei

Acknowledgements

With special thanks to Bill Kelly, Duncan Stearn and Eric Bossieux.

Table of Contents

Introduction

The National Congress of the Chinese Communist Party is held every five years in the Great Hall of the People in Beijing. The stage is always dominated by the classic symbol of communism: the hammer and sickle. When Chinese leaders host foreign dignitaries for state visits or international gatherings, the backdrop is completely different. Rather than the hammer and sickle, we see a monumental view of a mountainous landscape partly shrouded by mist. In the middle of the landscape is a waterfall pouring water from the mountains into the river below.

Like the hammer and sickle, the landscape is symbolic. In classic Chinese art, this image is known as a water-mountain picture. Water-mountain represents the Chinese view of Creation. Water is yin, mountain is yang. The ancient Chinese said: "When the yin and the yang, initially united, separated forever, the mountains poured forth water." The mysterious something that governed the separation of yin and yang is symbolized by the dragon, that most Chinese of all Chinese symbols. Today,

China combines a Western ideology and the rediscovery of its own ancient and unique world view to create a modern state.

Growing up in the West, we have a basic knowledge of the broad contours of global history. Europe began its colonial march in the 16th century, launched the scientific revolution in the 17th century, and was the world's political, scientific and cultural center of gravity for more than 400 years. The first tentative challenge to European leadership came in the second half of the 19th century, when Japan became the first independent country in the world to "copy" the Western approach to science, governance, law and education. Much of the rest of the world remained in the grip of colonialism and had to wait until the end of World War II to follow Japan's example. What history usually doesn't tell us is the other side of this story: while European science and technology helped Japan to modernize, Japanese art - based on the Chinese prototype - helped Europe to modernize its art and architecture and offered a potential model for the development of a "machine aesthetic."

In the 1850s, Japan began exporting to the West the quaint products of its traditional culture. It included delicate porcelain protected by unusual wrapping paper; colorful woodblock prints depicting daily life in 17th and 18th century Japan. The Japanese considered them as mere posters, rather than high art, which explains their use as wrapping paper. But in France, artists Manet, Monet and Renoir looking for an alternative for the traditional, optical style of European painting, became captivated by the Japanese prints. These prints could not be more different from Europe's photo-realistic style of painting developed during the Renaissance and perfected by classic masters like Da Vinci and Rembrandt.

Traditional European optical was based on two pictorial techniques: clair-obscur, or chiaroscuro (the effect of light and shadow) and linear perspective. Under the influence of the Japanese print, the early modernists eliminated all traces of clair-obscur from their paintings. Their work, later referred to as Impressionism, became a tapestry of pure color. However, the early modernists did not recognize that the Japanese print artists used a Chinese alternative for linear perspective. It came to be known in the West as axonometry. In the history of art, only two cultures developed a pictorial projection system to depict a "coherent" pictorial space on the two-dimensional picture plane - Europe and China.

In Part II we will see how European artists struggle to recognize the Chinese system. Understanding axonometry is understanding the birth of modern architecture.

Another and most curious encounter between the East and the West sheds more light on how our modern world developed. In the 17th century, the German polymath Gottfried Leibniz invented the numerical binary code that came to be used in modern, "digital" computers. A few years after announcing his invention, Leibniz wrote another paper on the subject and wrote that the Chinese should be credited with having invented the first binary code.

Leibniz first announced his invention in an article entitled 'Explanation of Binary Arithmetic' in 1679. His invention of the binary code was part of an attempt to design a mechanical calculator. Using two instead of 10 digits would simplify the design and the machine would require fewer parts. Our common decimal system is based on 10 digits. Higher numbers, 10 and above, are based on the power of 10 (10, 100, 1000). Leibniz substituted the 10 digits of the decimal system with 0 and 1, and substituted the power of 10 with the power of two. Thus the binary number 1010 represented (from right to left) 0 + 2 + 0 + 8 = decimal 10; the binary number 1111 represented 1 + 2 + 4 + 8 = decimal 15.

Leibniz was one of the first European thinkers with an interest in China and sent his first paper on the binary code to Father Joachim Bouvet, a French Jesuit missionary in Beijing, who was focusing his research in China on the I Ching (Book of Changes). Father Bouvet replied by telling Leibniz the Chinese had long used the binary code as it is the basis of what he called the Cova, the eight trigrams that form the basis of the 64 hexagrams used in the Book of Changes. Father Bouvet explained that the broken and unbroken lines that make up the trigrams and hexagrams are the same as the 0 and 1 of the binary code. Leibniz was elated and wrote his second paper on the origin of the Chinese binary code.

Fuxi (or Fu Hsi), Leibniz explained, is an ancient mythological ruler credited with having invented the Eight Trigrams. Leibniz wrote: "What is amazing in this reckoning is that this arithmetic by 0 and 1 is found to contain the mystery of the lines of an ancient King and philosopher named Fuxi, who is believed to have lived more than 4000 years ago, and whom the Chinese regard as the founder of their empire and their sciences."

Leibniz assumed the Chinese had lost the meaning of the Cova and that the true explanation of the Chinese code now had to come from Europeans. "Writing to me on 14 November 1701, [Father Bouvet] sent me this philosophical prince's grand figure, which goes up to 64, and leaves no further room to doubt the truth of our interpretation, such that it can be said that this Father has deciphered the enigma of Fuxi with the help of what I had communicated to him. And as these figures are perhaps the most ancient monument of science which exists in the world, this restitution of their meaning, after such a great interval of time, will seem all the more curious."

Historians have generally treated Leibniz's claim as a curious historical footnote. But a closer look at this fascinating story will show he was on the right track, which is all the more remarkable because he had no way of knowing that the 19th century mathematician George

Boole would develop an algebra of classes and the 10th century American scientist Claude Shannon, like the Chinese before him, would realize that a binary string can be given any arbitrary value, whether a letter, a picture or sound. The Chinese trigrams and hexagrams are the equivalent of Boolean classes; and they have the "arbitrary" attributes that Shannon referred to. Shannon made us realize a crucial point: A code is just a code. What matters is the attributes we give them and that we have agreement on their meaning. In Part III we will recount the remarkable history of the binary code in China and Europe.

There is one more thing. Much of our culture is, by definition, based on human constructs. Our minds create constructs as tools to achieve a certain goal or solve a given problem. An example is linear perspective, the graphic device to depict space on the picture plane. In a painting using linear perspective, the lines of projection into the distance converge at a point on the horizon. It convinces us we are looking at a coherent pictorial space, yet we know the vanishing point and the horizon are illusionary. They have no independent existence because they are a human construct. The same is true of the binary code. It is a human construct designed to help us with a specific task of solve a specific problem.

The advent of digital computers highlighted the dichotomy between digital and analog. The first computers were analog rather than digital, but computer scientists are realizing digital computers have limitations because they lack an analog quality. Like linear perspective, our distinction between analog and digital is valuable, but it a human construct. By themselves, they have no independent existence in reality. We may be able to get a better understanding of this issue when we look at the story of Leibniz and the digital revolution by combining the views of art and science. The dichotomy between analog and digital is one of the most important issues confronting artificial intelligence.

Western fascination with "the East" started in the 19th century and grew after World War II. Much of popular perception of the "East" made only a cursory distinction between India and China. As we shall see, this distinction is crucial and explains why China rather than India is first in line to take over the role as the most influential country in the world. This sequence has political, economic and cultural implications. China is a hybrid socialist-capitalist nation, India is a democracy, but in the coming decades China will have far greater influence on India and the world than India on China. It suggests that culture plays a larger role in the development of human history than is usually assumed.

PART I: A global consciousness

"We will begin with the basic contrast of spirit and matter. In the west the gulf between them has been impassable. For us spirit belongs to the life of prayer and worship, matter is the concern of science. This has directed our art to the extremes of religious meaning and naturalistic representation. The Chinese, by not carrying the empirical method far enough, failed to develop the natural sciences; and, by not pursuing the nature of spirit to the ultimate personal God, they never evolved a real religion in our sense of that word. Instead, the Chinese created a unique conception of the realm of the spirit which was one with the realm of matter. This meant that their painting would never become as religious, imitative, or personally expressive as our painting; and it also meant that art would become the prime vehicle for man's most profound thoughts and feelings about the mystery of the universe. This unique conception of spirit and matter was embodied in the notion of Tao."

George Rowley, *Principles of Chinese Painting* (1947)

1. Reconciling spirit and matter

Why is it that China rather than India is poised to replace the West as the leading region in the world? What gives China precedence over India? The most likely answer is the cultural difference between India and China. Democratic Japan and socialist China, politically different but culturally related, have been equally successful in assimilating and applying Western science to become advanced economies and technological giants.

The Western world has usually seen India and China as part of the "spiritual East." This view tends to overlook an important historical detail: Buddhism, an offspring of Hinduism, penetrated China, but the notion of Tao did not penetrate India. Tao had already shaped the Chinese world view when Buddhism arrived from India in the First Century. The foundations of China's social structure, its view of nature, its architecture, its art and its cosmogony were developed long before the first Buddhists made their way to China. When we look at the history of art and science, in both East and West, we see Tao not only shaped Chinese culture, but also had an indirect influence on the development of modern

Western art and architecture. The Chinese view of nature also anticipated modern scientific development, most notably the harnessing of electricity in the 19th century.

Civilizations began to develop after humanity emerged from its animist roots. Animists throughout the world perceived reality as an undifferentiated whole, with everything and every phenomenon permeated by spirits. For reason not quite clear, people in various regions and with varying speeds began making a distinction between "spirit" and "matter." It coincided with the evolutionary development of individual human consciousness. The three large source cultures in the world today, India, China and Europe, developed different views of what constitutes spirit and matter, and the terminology they used was a first indication of these differences.

In ancient India, the Sāmkhya philosophy sees the universe as consisting of two realities: Purusa (consciousness) and Prakriti (matter). The different strands of Indian spirituality focused on notions like pure consciousness, overcoming ego, the evolution of the soul and Ultimate Reality. Deities symbolized various aspects of the development of spiritual life. In the West the debate was shaped by Aristotle's study of physics (the knowledge of nature). His editor Andronicus of Rhodes classified Aristotle's later chapters as metaphysics (literally after or beyond physics). This notion framed the European philosophical debate on spirit and matter.

For the Chinese, the notion of Tao was the point of departure. First there was Tao, the unknowable universe, and then there was human. The Chinese concluded that Tao is based on a binary principle - Heaven and Earth, positive and negative, active and passive, growth and decay, etc. - and that humans should identify these polarities in all its manifestations in order to "insert" itself in the binary structure of nature with the least amount of friction. In the world of Tao there were no consoling or inspiring deities, only the stark reality of nature.

Historians offer various theories on why Europe rather than India, China or other regions of the world developed modern science. Some argue it was the Portuguese penetration of the Indian Ocean by Vasco da Gama in 1498. Others point at the development of modern science starting with

Copernicus, Galileo and Newton. Still others mention Descartes as the key figure in the scientific revolution. One factor most agree on is that Europe went further than other cultures in advancing the empirical method, relying on experiments validated by measurement tools, together with the scientific concept of proof. This concept made it possible to separate facts from belief, crucial in the development of science and technology.

2. *Qi* and electromagnetism

Of all European inventions, the harnessing of electromagnetism was arguably the most consequential. It relied on earlier scientific developments but electricity made all modern scientific and technological developments possible: electric light, the telegraph, ignition systems for internal combustion, x-rays, large-scale industrial production and avionics. Electricity also enabled the development of quantum physics, used by scientists to crack the mysteries of nature on a subatomic level. Moreover, quantum physics confirmed the ancient animist notion that everything is intrinsically related.

The harnessing of electricity also validated the old Chinese notion of Tao, the idea nature is a polar phenomenon governed by complementary opposites that have a mutual attraction and are interdependent. Tao was a "prescientific" understanding of electromagnetism. The Chinese referred to the tension between the polarities as *qi*. The word has various meanings, but as a natural phenomenon and manifestation of Tao, it can be easily visualized. Float a needle between two magnets and the needle will settle at the point where the tension is most acute. That point is *qi*. Joseph Needham, author of the monumental *Science and Civilization in China*, translated *qi* as "matter-energy", a term derived from quantum physics.

Identifying Tao enabled the Chinese to evolve from animism while retaining an awareness of the omnipresence of nature. The ancient Chinese made it an art, if not a science, to identify all conceivable opposites they recognized in nature: growth and decay, strong and weak, far and near, horizontal and vertical, space and time, etc., and they made the reconciliation of opposites the guiding principle in the development of their civilization. Confucianism is one of many "products" of

Tao, as is Chinese architecture, agriculture, martial arts, medicine, music and dietary habits.

3. Prelude to New Age

Seen from the West, with its scientific world view, it was not surprising that Asia as a whole was regarded as "the spiritual East." Eastern spirituality became a catch-all phrase for all Asian religious and spiritual traditions. Indian thought is rich and complex and influenced China, but the historical development explains China's distinct development: First there was Tao and the *I Ching* (about 3000 BCE), then Tao-inspired Confucianism (600 BCE), then Buddhism's introduction into China (200 BCE), and then the founding of the Taoist religion (200 BCE), possibly instituted by Chinese thinkers concerned by the popularity of Buddhism and the fear the Chinese would lose sight of the Tao – and the here and now. Unlike Buddhism, Tao in its original form offered no consolation or a heavenly hereafter.

Gottfried Leibniz was among the first Western thinkers to study Eastern thought, followed by the so-called German romantics and, in the 19th century, by Arthur Schopenhauer, Ralph Waldo Emerson and

Henry David Thoreau. Western scholars translated the Bhagavad Gita, Samkhya Karika, Upanishads and other Indian classics. The *I Ching* was translated into Latin as early as 1730 and in German by 1830.

Starting in the 18th century, the West discovered the East as a rich source of spiritual inspiration. Russian-born Helena (Madam) Blavatsky, cofounder of the Theosophical Society, popularized Eastern spirituality with her book *The Secret Doctrine: The Synthesis of Science, Religion and Philosophy*, a commentary on what she claimed were ancient Tibetan manuscripts. According to Blavatsky, The Secret Doctrine was "the accumulated wisdom of the age… the uninterrupted record covering thousands of generations of Seers whose respective experiences were made to test and to verify the traditions passed orally by one early race to another, of the teachings of higher and exalted beings, who watched over the childhood of Humanity."

In the first half of the 20th century, interest in Eastern spirituality was mostly confined to Western intellectuals, artists and (quantum) physicists, but in the 1950s it penetrated popular consciousness. American writers like

Allen Ginsberg and Jack Kerouac of the so-called Beat Generation rejected Western "materialism" and explored Eastern religions. They experimented with psychedelic drugs, championed non-conformity and set the stage for the New Age movement. In the 1970s and 1980s, several books further popularized Eastern spirituality and cosmogony. They had in common the idea the East offered the West spiritual insights that were confirmed by modern (quantum) physics. Popular among these books were Fritjof Capra's *The Tao of Physics: An Exploration of the Parallels Between Modern Physics and Eastern Mysticism* and Gary Zukav's *The Dancing Wu Li Masters*.

Following Carl Jung early in the 20th century, Western psychology also studied Eastern thought to help them to understand the subconscious, and they developed models that integrated Western psychology with insights from Eastern, mostly Indian spirituality.

4. Original sources versus interpretations

Ancient Chinese and Indian thought accumulated an enormous amount of commentary and interpretation, but the originating texts suggest an early and profound understanding of human psychology. The original corpus of the *I Ching*, perhaps written more than 4000 years ago, uses binary opposites to awaken the human conscience, and to show that the question we ask contains the seed of the answer. We already know the answer but we are made aware of it by consulting the *I Ching*. Abstractly, it applies the polarity of nature to human perceptions of reality in order to help readers to identify the balance between binary opposites. The original corpus has no reference to either Tao or yin and yang. It only refers to abstract opposites like positive and negative, advancing and retreating, remorse and humiliation, favorable and unfavorable, and makes no claims to know the spiritual Holy Grail of "ultimate reality."

The oldest Hindu texts also have a psychological dimension. Indian sages "classified" humanity in four generic types: spiritual seeker, warrior, merchant and worker. The generic caste type is the first example of what we today would call psychological profiling. Each human being, both male and female, has characteristics of all four castes in various degrees, but one of the four caste types usually dominates in each individual. The Vedas claim the four castes "take turns in ruling the world," meaning each caste is the prominent caste at a given era (*yuga*) in an everlasting cycle.

The American futurist Lawrence Taub uses the Veda's notion of caste to integrate the Hindu concept of eternal, cyclical time with the Western notion of linear time. In his book *The Spiritual Imperative: Sex, Age and Caste move the Future*, Taub argues humanity goes only through one caste cycle rather than an endless cosmic cycle. He correlates the rise and fall of each of the four castes with concrete historical periods. In Taub's model, humanity has just emerged from the Merchant Caste Age, during which the West was the most prominent region in the world, because the West as a whole most closely fits the psychological profile of the merchant type. Humanity is now moving into the Worker Caste Age, in which East Asia replaces the West as the world's most influential region, and for the same reason: it most closely matches the psychological profile of the worker caste.

The "look East" movement that started in the 19th century was fueled by Western intellectuals who felt they had exhausted Western traditions in philosophy, religion and even art – everything from Christian dogmas to Newtonian mechanics and Cartesian dualism. The European world view seemed limited in its ability to explain modern scientific and social developments and blocked more global perspectives. It manifested itself in theoretical physics, Jungian psychology, literature, and arts. Eastern traditions offered new vistas for understanding the world. Integrating Eastern and Western world views became a key driver of the New Age movement.

5. Emergence of global consciousness

The look-East movement in the West stimulated an interest in Eastern spiritual practices like yoga, meditation and Tantra. The subtext was usually that the materialistic West could learn from the spiritual East. But the reverse was also true. The spiritual East had a lot to learn from the "materialistic" West. The West had produced not only advanced sciences but also economic and political theories necessary for the transition from agricultural to industrial society. It they developed the notion of individualism, workers rights and human rights and life-saving medical sciences. Eastern thinkers realized they had to learn from the

West in order to develop modern and prosperous societies.

Japan was the first Asia country to assimilate the ways of the West, albeit reluctantly. As only one of two countries in Asia to escape colonization (together with Thailand), Japan had been quite content to maintain its 200-year policy of national isolation, imposed in the 17th century to avoid colonization by the Western merchant powers. In 1844 the King of The Netherlands asked Japan to open its borders for international trade but the Japanese declined. Nine years later, the American government sent steam-powered warships from the United States Navy into Tokyo Bay and demanded access to Japanese ports. The Japanese rulers, still adhering to the Samurai code of using only swords to defend oneself honorably, understood times had changed.

The Japanese set out on a rapid modernization program. They sent their best and brightest to the West to take an inventory of Western science, governmental systems and educational institutions. Showing their pragmatism, they opted for an a la carte approach: a British-style parliament, a combination of German and French civil law, the British telegraph system, German-style mandatory education and conscription and German medicine. After World War II, which ended colonialism, most other countries in Asia followed Japan's example, with varying decrees of speed and success. East Asia clearly outpaced West Asia, but the products of Western civilization, from railroads and electricity to modern political ideology, gradually penetrated all corners of Asia.

6. Ideology as a means to an end

The spread of technology and Western concepts and globalization is leading to shared global experiences and the first baby steps toward a global consciousness. Eastern spirituality impacts the West, and Western culture, science and technology changes the worldview of the East. Both impact the rest of the world through cross-fertilization. Cultural, industrial and technological practices are often re-imported after having been modified abroad. Western psychology integrates spiritual insights from India and developed transpersonal psychology which is now used all over the world, including India. In industry, Japan's "application technology" (efficient manufacturing based on the US-invented "just-in-time" system), reverberated around the world and forced the major restructuring of Western economies and industries. India, despite millions of people lacking basic human needs, is one of the largest producers of software, and even the poorest of Indians access American and Japanese social media platforms through mobile phones.

Developments over the past 50 years illustrate why conventional Western ideology and economic theories are no longer the most useful frameworks for understanding the world. Japan and China, one nominally democratic and the other nominally communist, are equally successful in applying Western science and technology to develop modern societies. Together with South Korea, they have become "the factory of the world." If the socialist-capitalist system applied in China is more effective than a democratic-capitalist system applied in many other advanced countries, where does it leave conventional notions about economics and political ideology as a model for developing countries? If modern East Asia doesn't completely upend conventional theory about ideology and economics, it limits their blanket global applicability.

PART I: A GLOBAL CONSCIOUSNESS

People raised in relative affluence in Western society may view East Asia as overly concerned with economic development and material progress, and they decry the loss of traditional values. People emerging from generations of poverty, colonialism or political instability obviously have different concerns. To them, ideology is a means to an end, not an end in itself. We can only speculate on how China will impact the world in the next decades. Our only point of reference is the rise of Japan in the 1980s. Japan forced the restructuring of the global economy with its highly efficient production. Most people in the developed world used Japanese products in their daily lives, and the products of Japanese culture influenced everything from industrial design to fashion.

China's population is ten times the size of Japan, its geographic size 25 times later. Its potential influence is not just economic. As a "source culture," and forced to find a guiding principle for its newfound power, it will have to look at its own deep history and its own native world view. This is cause for optimism. The notion of Tao asks for the reconciliation op opposites, including spirit and matter. When applied to the task of wrestling a civilization from "unruly" nature, this leads to an approach where the distinction between ethics and aesthetics dissolves. In traditional China, the lines between art and life were never clear, even in the most mundane aspects. Medical practitioners wrote prescriptions for patients in verse. Industrialization may seem to have obscured China's aesthetic outlook on life, but its roots are deep and as old as the *I Ching* and will re-emerge when the timing is right.

* * *

PART II: A global architecture

No more valuable object lesson was ever afforded civilization than this instance of a people who have made of their land and the buildings upon it, of there gardens, their manners and garb, their utensils, adornments, and their very gods, a single consistence whole, a unit inspired by a living sympathy with Nature, spontaneous and inevitable. To the smallest fraction of Japanese lives what was divorced from Nature was reclaimed by Art, and so redeemed.

Frank Lloyd Wright, The Japanese print: An Interpretation

7. China and the modernization of the West

Japan started to modernize in the late 19th century by importing Western science and institutions. China did not follow until the second half of the 20th century. The enormous country was divided and weakened by Western powers until the 1940s and had a late start. After World War II the country was unified using Soviet-style Marxism, with all the excesses that usually accompany violent revolution. In the 1980s the country launched a hybrid system of socialism and capitalism and lifted 500 million people out of poverty in one generation, a feat no one had thought possible under a one-party rule that restricts personal freedom and democratic rights.

East Asia modernized in the 20th century, but so did Europe, and China and Japan played an unwitting but crucial role in Europe's own modernization. While East Asia assimilated the "natural sciences" of the West, the West assimilated what we may call the "natural aesthetics" of East Asia. With Vincent van Gogh and Frank Lloyd Wight as rare exceptions, the role of East Asia in the modernization of Western aesthetics was been largely overlooked, partly because the West attached great value to "originality" and because it had a latent condescension for non-European art. Europeans routinely classified the Japanese print as "primitive art."

While Europe based its arts of the appearance of nature, China and Japan based their art on the internal, "binary" principle of nature. This manifested itself in nearly all aspects of Chinese civilization, including axonometry, China's version of linear perspective and a crucial feature of Chinese architecture and painting. The underlying current in the development of modern art and architecture in the West between the 1860s and the 1920s was the search for an alternative to linear perspective and the ultimate embrace of axonometry.

In the 19th century, when the Industrial Revolution gathered steam, it became apparent that European traditional aesthetics in arts, design and especially architecture, "the mother of all the arts," were ill-suited to the emerging Machine Age. Classic Western aesthetics has its roots in the sculptural traditions of Greek architecture. Greek builders, like their Egyptian predecessors, were sculptors. They sculpted large stones to make columns for temples and the sculptural elements of the entablature: architrave, frieze and cornice. Technically, this approach to architecture is known as the load-and-support system. It lacked structure in that it relied on weight (gravity) to remain standing. Some early Greek temples had columns sculpted in the form of female figures (caryatid), most famously the Caryatid Porch of the Erechtheion in Athens build between 421 and 407 BCE.

Greece's sculptural load-and-support system was the model for the subsequent development of European architecture. In the 1st century BCE, the Roman architect Vitruvius codified European architecture on the basis of Greek anthropomorphic principles. Vitruvius used the human figure as the principle source of proportions in the classical order of architecture: The foot is one-seventh of the height of a man, hence the height of a column should be seven times its diameter. Leonardo da Vinci immortalized "Vitruvian Man" with the drawing of the human figure with outstretched arms in a geometric figure of a square and a circle. Vitruvius' architectural canons dominated European architecture until the early 20th century. But the Industrial Revolution forced architects to rethink traditional architecture. Its sculptural aesthetic was unsuited for the construction of large factories and industrially-produced building materials like structural steel and concrete. Architects and engineers needed a new style suited for the modern era. They needed a "machine aesthetic."

8. Japan as intermediary

Europe's 19th century painters had other, if related, concerns. Starting in France in the second half of the 19th century, rebellious

French artists tried to break the hold on art by the "Academy", the official arbitrator of art. The social-minded Barbizon school had already turned its back on the Salon art of Paris, which primarily served to satisfy the bourgeoisie with vain portraiture in optical detail. Barbizon artists depicted struggling farmers at their back-breaking work in the fields to highlight social inequality, an issue also addressed by the revolutionary economist Karl Marx. The French art establishment derided the Barbizon school artists as "socialists who don't wash their linen."

The Barbizon rebellion was rooted in the prevailing social injustice, but another front would be opened against the establishment. It was an aesthetic rebellion fueled by Japanese art. In the 1860s, modern-minded artists in France discovered Japanese wood block prints. These small, unpretentious pictures depicted life in 18th and 19th century Japan. The Japanese regarded the prints as a plebian art. It explained why the prints arrived in Europe unceremoniously as wrapping paper for Japanese porcelain, one of Japan's first exports after it opened up to the world. But European artists recognized something special in these unpretentious prints – their visual immediacy.

The Japanese prints had no shadows or apparent light source. The light in the pictures seemed internal. The prints suggested pictorial space and depth (3D) but did not have the "suction effect" of the vanishing point, the principle feature of linear perspective that governed European painting. While the picture suggested space, the human figures depicted in the prints were flat (2D). The Japanese print artists outlined the figures with flowing calligraphic strokes and filled them with flat, unmodulated color. To the European eye conditioned by optical representation these images used a pictorial language that seemed from a different world. By 1880, nearly all modern-minded artists in France – Manet, Degas, Renoir, Monet, Pissarro and others, later referred to as the Impressionists – collected and even copied prints from popular Japanese print masters like Utamaro, Hokusai and Hiroshige.

Whether the Japanese prints were the catalyst for the Impressionist revolution or reinforced the rebellion against the official Academy, the result was a frontal assault on traditional pictorial conventions that had dominated European painting since the Renaissance and its optical roots in ancient

Greece. The work of the early Impressionist still showed traces of the optical approach of traditional European painting, but the dark bitumen shadows of clair-obscur disappeared from Impressionist painting. If shadows were depicted at all, they were rendered in various hues of color.

9. Van Gogh arrives in Paris

The Impressionist revolution was in its second decade when Vincent van Gogh arrived in Paris from his native Holland. Van Gogh's last major work from his Dutch period was the Potato Eaters, a large, somber scene of a farmer's family in a shack having a meal under petroleum light. Pitch-black shadows dominated the mood in the painting. Before arriving in Paris, Van Gogh believed the Barbizon school was the avant-garde in French painting. When he saw the work of the Impressionists, he realized the avant-garde had taken a completely different, aesthetic direction. Gone were the struggling farmers in the fields under grey skies. The Impressionists depicted the gay life in the city in tapestries of bright colors.

Van Gogh realized the Japanese print had kick-started a revolution in painting and he and his brother Theo, an art dealer in Paris, started collecting these Japanese prints. As if to internalize the methods of the Japanese print masters, Van Gogh copied several prints in oil and canvas. He wrote a letter to his sister in Holland about the new direction art had taken in Paris: "You may understand the change in painting when you think for example of the Japanese pictures one sees everywhere. Theo and I have hundreds of these Japanese prints." Before even attempting to show his own work, Van Gogh organized an exhibition of his collection of Japanese prints in a café in Paris.

The Japanese print had given Van Gogh the impression Japan was a country permanently bathing in sunshine and he moved to the south of France hoping to be inspired by a similarly bright environment. Once in the French Midi he would create the images that made him a legend: the Harvest at La Crau, The Bridge at Arles, and the iconic Sunflowers. Like the Japanese print, the Sunflowers has no apparent light source and no shadows. The light in the picture is "internal." Rather than an optical facsimile of real sunflowers, the Sunflowers is a reality in its own right.

Van Gogh's Sunflowers is an iconic image of the Modernist Revolution and the departure from Europe's optical tradition in art. But the Japanese prints had another "modern" feature, one that was overlooked by the early modernist. The Japanese print masters, rather than using linear perspective, used a pictorial projection system know as axonometry. The projection device originated in China some 2000 years ago, and its value would not be recognized until the 1920s, during the climax of the Modernist Revolution, when artists became architects and architects became artists.

10. Frank Lloyd Wright: The First Architect

The only Modernist more vocal about the Japanese role in the modernization of Western aesthetics was the American architect Frank Lloyd Wright. Wright's role in the development of modern architecture was so great that he is often referred to as "the first architect." Like Van Gogh, Wright was an avid collector of Japanese prints. He covered the wall of his first office with Japanese prints and would later publish a book featuring prints from his own collection. "If the Japanese print were to be deducted from my education," he told an audience later in life, "I don't know what direction the whole might have taken."

America discovered Japan in the years following the opening of Japan to international trade. In 1876 Japan participated in the World Expo in Philadelphia and brought its own pavilion – a temple from Kyoto. The wooden structure had been disassembled in Japan, and its components – pillars, beams, panels, tatami mats and sliding doors – were packed and shipped across the Pacific. Once reassembled in Philadelphia, the building attracted immediate attention from American architects. They were amazed by the standardized components, its modularity, and its open floor plan. The unassuming building seemed both old and modern at the same time.

In 1893, the Japanese erected the same pavilion at the Chicago Expo, and one of the visitors was Chicago-native Frank Lloyd Wright. Wright also noticed the structural quality of the Japanese building. The building appeared to have been designed from the inside out. This was in contrast with tradition European architecture, which typically started with the external shape of building. Wright became captivated by Japan, started collecting

Japanese prints and traveled to Japan several times. At the turn of the century he built a series of residential homes called Prairie Houses that echoed traditional Japanese architecture. The homes had a horizontal slant, overhanging eaves, open floor plans and doors that opened directly to the garden outside. Wright designed the homes from the inside out, rather than from the outside in. The spatial needs of the occupant determined the floor plan, which in turn determined the shape of the house. To convey the idea that he designed his homes from the inside out, Wright called his approach "organic."

The modular structure of Japanese architecture was characterized by flat, rectangular planes. This made it an ideal model for concrete, a new building material. Some of Wright's famous Prairie House designs, like the Ward Willets House, use similar rectangular planes and resemble famous Japanese buildings like Katsura Villa. Most importantly, Wright had noticed that Japanese architecture demonstrated an acute aesthetic awareness of space. Edgar Tafel, one of Wright's apprentices, later recalled that Wright often referred to Japanese architecture when discussing architectural space. "The Japanese house, with its sliding screens, gives a unique sense of movable space. With each rearrangement of the screens we become aware of the 'shape of the space', or, like the Japanese print, of merely an interruption of space, a moment in space. Imagine the surprise he experienced when by chance he came across a quotation from Laozi (Lao Tzu): 'The reality of the building does not consist of the four walls and the roof but the space to be lived in.'"

Wright's revolutionary Prairie Homes caused a sensation the world over and had great influence on the development of modern architecture in Europe. Wright gracefully acknowledged the artistic debt he owed to Japan and found it puzzling the pioneers of modernism in Europe failed to acknowledge this debt. In his book *The Japanese Print: An Interpretation* he wrote: "The lesson of the Japanese print came home to me as it did to the European painters who developed Cubism and Futurism. It [the print] lies intrinsically at the root of all this so-called modernism. Strangely unnoticed, uncredited."

11. Mother of All Arts

The "modern" qualities of the Japanese print were based on the Chinese prototype, and the same is true of Japanese architecture. Its modularity, structural principles and awareness of space date back to the first millennium BCE. In ancient China we see why architecture has been called the mother of all arts. Chinese emperors, when they ascended the "Dragon Throne" (the dragon symbolizes Tao) usually built entirely new capitals. The cities were laid out in a checkerboard pattern divided into nine quarters (modules). The royal quarter occupied the cell in the center of the upper row of the grid. The other eight modules were subdivided in nine smaller modules or wards. The palace, temples, government building, private residences and markets were all designed to fit into the modularized grid. Some ancient Chinese cities were 10 kilometers to a side covering 100 square kilometers. The construction of the cities, all using standardized, prefabricated building components assembled on site, had all the features of an industrial process, except machines.

The nine-square grid was based on an ancient diagram called Luoshu (well-field). Legend has it that ancient China suffered an enormous deluge when a turtle emerged from the water with a nine-square pattern on its back. The finders saw it as an omen and gave the shell of the turtle to (pre-historic) Emperor Yu, who used it to design defenses against the water. The nine-square grid was used as for the layout of the Mintang, a "cosmic observatory" to help Chinese rulers to navigate the ship of state through cosmological changes.

The nine-field layout of the Luoshu served as the blueprint for China's overall "architecture complex," which both determined and reflected its social structure. It was used for the division of land, the production of rice and the organization of communities. Mencius, critic of Confucius, referred to the nine-field grid when he described agricultural compounds. He wrote: "I would ask you, if the country where the nine-square division is observed, to reserve one division to be cultivated on the system of mutual aid, [would this not deserve consideration?] ... The central square is the public field, and the eight families, each having its private hundred acres, cultivate this public field in common. And not till public work is finished may they presume to attend to their private affairs." The modern Chinese historian Feng Yu-lan pointed out that Mencius' proposal had "socialist implications."

China's ancient cities were both a living environment and a frame for its social system. The size of buildings, internal division and architectural decorations were determined by the social status of their occupants as early as the 6th century BCE. We can only marvel at the organizational skill of the Chinese. The ancient city of Daxing, a metropolis of 84 square kilometers built in the 6th century CE, was "...ready for occupancy in one year." Only standardized architecture and prefabrication made it possible to build cities of this size with such speed. It also required commonly understood building practices that had been handed down through the generations. The Chinese had their own "Vitruvius" in the (mythological) Lu Ban, the Patron Saint of Chinese carpenters and builders. They evoked Lu Ban before commencing work:

The two words 'yin' and 'yang' must come in the first place,
Then the construction work will advance well.
In the nine spheres of the hall with nine purlins and five bays,
There will be perpetual luck for a thousand years and ten thousand years.

Careful adherence to the true measures of our Patron Saint,
Will bring for the wealth and rank, and ample farmland as well.
If the people of the present age do not obey
The methods of the immortal (master Lu Ban),
Disharmony between the house and its occupants will be the result.

Designing and building a city of 100 square kilometers within a year required many skills, including drafting skills to draw the city in whole or in part on paper. In Europe architects relied on linear perspective to render their architectural conception. The Chinese used a projection system they called *dengjiao toushi* or "equal-angle see-through," later known as axonometry in the West. An axonometric projection is essential for depicting buildings with uniform dimensions. Parallel lines, whether horizontal, vertical or diagonal, must be parallel. This unique quality of axonometry explains why it was invented by builders rather than artists. Only later did Chinese artists use axonometry in painting, including the hand scroll, the only pictorial art format in the world that depicts a story in space and time. Linear perspective, which relies on the fixed vantage point of the observer, is a static moment in time and cannot be used in the pictorial representation of space and time.

PART II: A GLOBAL ARCHITECTURE

12. Linear perspective and Chinese axonometry

Axonometry was to Chinese (and Japanese) art what linear perspective was to Western art. In the early days of the Renaissance, European artists used Greek optics and Euclidean geometry to develop linear perspective to depict a coherent 3D space on the 2D picture plane. Medieval art made attempts to structure pictorial space but failed to make the space coherent. The breakthrough came with the invention of the vanishing point. In its basic form, linear perspective shows lines that are perpendicular to the picture place receding to a fixed point at the horizon, like the tracks of a railroad seemingly converging in the distance. Both the horizon and the vanishing point are illusionary. They do not exist in reality. Moreover, linear perspective is bound to the terrestrial plane. It cannot be detached from the horizon. This is unlike axonometry, which can be used in outer space and can "depict" infinity – or at least the illusion of infinity in the mind of the viewer.

When the early European modernists, the Impressionist, moved away from optical representation, they were confronted with a dilemma. Optical depiction relies on two pictorial techniques: clair-obscur and linear perspective. Under the influence of the Japanese wood block print, the modernist moved away from clair-obscur, the pictorial means to gives 3D objects the illusion of volume on the 2D picture plane. When the early modernists removed the illusion of plastic (3D) form from their paintings, linear perspective became conceptually problematic. In many Impressionist landscapes, we see the artists used various ways to "flatten" pictorial space. They often focused on suppressing the "suction effect" of the vanishing point. Examples are Van Gogh's Harvest in La Crau and Cezanne's Mont Sainte-Victoire. Both artists "restructured" pictorial space to bring the visual information of the image closer to the surface of the picture plane.

The struggle with linear perspective took an improbable turn with the Cubists in the early 20th century. Cezanne, in his attempt to restructure pictorial space, had painted several still lives that included objects like vases and fruit baskets that appeared to be depicted from different vantage points. Despite this apparent incongruity, the space in Cezanne's paintings remained reasonable coherent. Art historian

Erle Loran, in his book *Cezanne's Compositions*, used diagrams to show the objects in Cezanne's painting seems to incorporate several vantage points and may have caught the eye of Pablo Picasso. In his seminal Cubist painting Les Demoiselles d'Avignon, a scene in a brothel showing five nude female figures, Picasso depicted one of the females ostensibly seen from different vantage points at the same time. In other words, Picasso seemingly combined different views of a three-dimensional object in one single form.

Picasso, like Cezanne before him, remained silent on his pictorial experiment. But depicting different views of a plastic object in a single form confused painting and sculpture. A sculpture is 3D and can be viewed in time from different vantage points. A painting is by definition 2D and, unless it is a Chinese hand scroll, can only depict a frozen moment in time. We can suggest movement in a painting, as the Futurist did, but trying to depict the notion of time in a painting is a conceptual and aesthetic incongruity. Caught up in the excitement of the Modernist Revolution, art critics and theorists offered various interpretations for the Cubists experiments. Prominent art critic Guillaume Apollinaire praised the Cubists for their attempt "to get rid of perspective, of that miserable tricky perspective, of that fourth dimension in reverse, of that infallible device for making all things shrink." Apollinaire referred to the vanishing point of linear perspective but this left readers in the dark about the meaning of "the fourth dimension in reverse."

Other critics resorted to non-Euclidian geometry to explain Cubism, apparently oblivious to the fact that non-Euclidian geometry, like the notion of the fourth dimension, deals with theoretical, mathematical space, not aesthetic, pictorial space. Still others drew parallels with Einstein's Relativity Theory, provoking the scientist to later distance himself from Cubism: "This new 'language' of art has nothing in common with the Theory of Relativity." In his book *The Life of a Painter*, Futurist artist Gini Severini later frankly admitted the modernists merely repeated what they heard in café's and that no one really understood the scientific theories.

The early modernists were unaware that an alternative to linear perspective was readily available. It had been used in China for centuries. The world knows only two graphic devices to create the illusion of a coherent space on the picture plane: European linear perspective and Chinese axonometry. Linear perspective did not have to be destroyed. It simply needed an alternative projection system that could deal with the demands of the technological and industrial era. And the only alternative was axonometry. The needed for a new, "objective" projection system explains why modernist architects working with industrially-produced building materials, rather than artists, recognize axonometry as an invaluable addition to linear perspective.

13. Artists and architect on common ground

In the 1920, modernist architects, in part inspired by Frank Lloyd Wright, elevated "the creation of space" as the essence of modern architecture. It was a conceptual departure from traditional Western architecture, which saw architecture as an art of (anthropological) form. In 1912, the Austrian-born American architect Rudolf Schindler wrote: "The architect has finally discovered the medium of his art: SPACE." Russian Suprematist artist Kazimir Malevich was captivated by space. He called himself "The President of SPACE." Dutch artist Theo van Doesburg wrote in 1916:

"The foundation of a building is space. Hence the visual consciousness of the architect ought to be based on Space."

Theo van Doesburg was the driving force behind De Stijl, an interdisciplinary art movement that included artists, architects, poets and graphic designers. Piet Mondrian was a founding member, and his work served as a blueprint for De Stijl's revolutionary architecture. Mondrian painted rectangular forms of unequal size that were perfectly balanced by the different visual weight of the primary colors red, blue and yellow. The images were meditations on equilibrium and could not be further removed from his illustrious compatriots and predecessors Rembrandt and Van Gogh. Mondrian claimed to have been inspired by The Secret Doctrine of Madam Blavatsky. Van Doesburg had reviewed a Mondrian exhibition in Amsterdam for an art magazine and wrote: "These works, which impress me with their elementary-pure artistic quality, remain calm and dignified under the derisive laughter of the public that only looks for what it knows. But art is what one doesn't know."

PART II: A GLOBAL ARCHITECTURE

Van Doesburg and De Stijl architect Cornelius van Eesteren took Mondrian's gridded images as a starting point for De Stijl's revolutionary architecture. They took Mondrian's grid and transformed it into three dimensions. De Stijl exhibited the designs in 1923 in Paris and caused a sensation in Europe, not in the least for the way they were depicted. Van Doesburg and Van Eesteren rendered the models using axonometry, the ancient projection system first used in the construction of China's ancient mega cities.

De Stijl's exhibition marked the breakthrough of axonometry in the West. In the following decades, the ancient Chinese projection system became part of the curriculum of architects and designers all over the world. Today axonometry is used to design everything from homes and offices to trains and space stations. It was also essential to the development of Computer Aided Design in the 1960s and all subsequent developments in visual computing. Our modern world is virtually designed in axonometry.

* * *

PART III: A global digital planet

If you wish to affirm what they deny and deny what they affirm, the best means is Illumination.

Zhuangzi

14. Logic of Boolean algebra

Punch the letter A on a keyboard and the computer will read 0100001. The binary number is part of the ASCII code (American Standard Code for Information Interchange) introduced in 1963 and is a global standard for alphanumerical symbols on computer keyboards. The ASCII code illustrates that a code is a mutual agreement and application of its meaning.

The same principle is at work in the Chinese binary code used in the *I Ching*. The broken and unbroken lines in the 64 hexagrams of the *I Ching* are binary representations of natural opposites the ancient Chinese identified in Nature: negative and positive, night and day, cold and hot, horizontal and vertical, retreating and advancing, female and male and an infinite number of other opposites. The trigrams and hexagrams are "gradations" of these opposites in discrete, binary steps. Attributes given to trigrams and hexagrams denote various states, conditions and tendencies the Chinese observed in Nature. The *I Ching* set the "standards" for this code and they have been used by the Chinese for well over 3000 years.

After Gottfried Leibniz developed the binary code at the end of the 17th century, he failed to secure funding for the development of his binary mechanical calculator. The binary code seemed doomed to be forgotten until the 19th century English mathematician George Boole recognized the value of its logic. Boole developed the algebra that carries his name, an invention that would become crucial to the modern information age. Boolean algebra enabled mathematicians for the first time to perform algebraic operations on groups or generic classes of objects usually not considered mathematical objects. A text book example of Boolean algebra is this: If the symbol x represents the class of all "white objects" and the symbol y the class of all "round objects," the symbol xy represents the class of objects that are simultaneously white and round. The notion of classed was also used by the inventor of the Chinese trigrams, which likewise represent classes, in the Chinese case classes of objects and processes that were purely or proportionally yin or yang.

To perform algebraic operations on these symbols, Boole invented several operators: AND, OR, NO, IF and THEN. This enabled mathematicians to add certain classes and exclude others: "hotdog AND mayonnaise OR ketchup NO salt." Boolean logic is simply a sequence of yes or no, true or false choices. There is no "maybe" – unless doubt is conditional on another probability or likelihood. "IF I get a raise, THEN I will buy a new car." As we shall see later, this logic would be crucial in cybernetics and its offspring artificial intelligence.

The value of Leibniz's binary code and Boolean algebra became apparent after the harnessing of electricity in the 19th century, leading to the development of the electric calculating machine, the forerunner of the modern computer. Early computers were analog machines. They relied on analogous variations in the strength of the electrical signal. In the 1930s scientists realized a binary system had distinct advantages over analog systems. Low current would be 0, high current 1, meaning binary systems only had to deal with two states: on and off. This made them less susceptible to variations in the strength of electrical current and thus more stable than analog machines.

In 1937, Claude Shannon published a landmark thesis called 'A Symbolic Analysis of Relay and Switching Circuits'. Shannon showed that Leibniz's binary code was perfectly suited for the implementation of Boolean logic in electrical circuits. The binary number 1 would denote "true" (yes, inside a class), 0 would be "false" (no, outside a class). Shannon was primarily concerned with solving mathematical problems of increasingly complex telephone switching circuits, but his paper provided the basis on which nearly all modern computers are built.

The second point Shannon made in his paper would earn him the epithet "Father of the Information Age." Shannon realized binary numbers could represent words, sounds, images and even abstract thoughts and ideas. All it required was a method of converting a binary number into an analog signal. One of the first implementations of this revolutionary idea came in 1961, when computer scientist John Kelly at Bell Labs demonstrated

Shannon's concept by programming a computer to output an analog audio signal. The song was made famous by the movie *2001: A Space Odyssey*. The menacing computer HAL (Heuristically programmed ALgorithmic computer) sang the song when its memory was unplugged. Today, binary numbers represent everything from multimedia to artificial intelligence systems.

15. Psychological computer

The application of the binary code in modern computers and the ancient binary code used in the *I Ching* may are based on the same logic: a code is just a code. It is the attributes given to the code that matter. If we agree on the meaning of the attribute, like the ASCII code, it becomes a "standard." The same principle is at work in the trigrams and hexagrams that form the basis of the *I Ching*. In the Chinese binary code, the broken lines denote all things generically classified as negative, the unbroken lines are all things considered to be positive. A combination of three broken and unbroken lines denotes gradations of negative and positive. The trigram of three broken lines denotes pure yin and stands for Earth, winter, horizontal, decay, retreating, etc.; the trigram of three unbroken lines denotes yang and stands for Heaven, summer, vertical, growth and advancing, etc. lines denotes spring or fall. Combinations of yin and yang lines denote transitional states or processes. Spring can be associated with the notion of advancing, autumn with the notion of withdrawing.

To create further gradations or subclasses, the Chinese combined the Eight Trigrams in all possible combinations to form the 64 hexagrams. The attributes associated with each trigram carried over into the hexagrams. The trigram for wind (also associated with wood) placed on top of the trigram for mountain, produced the hexagram "gradual advance." If we think of the effect of wind on a mountain, the attribute abstractly makes sense. The trigram for lake combined with the trigram for mountain conveys the notion of "mutual influence." All the other hexagrams convey similar qualities and tendencies, each the product of its two constituent trigrams and all based on tendencies and qualities rooted in natural processes.

The hexagrams are ancient equivalents of the modern barcode used in computerized processes. A barcode is a unique code for a specific product, process or condition. A hexagram is a barcode for a generic concept derived from Nature and human perceptions of natural processes. Interpreting the trigram and hexagrams requires understanding of the Chinese view of nature. Conversely, it also sheds light on how the Chinese perceived Nature and human psychology more than 4000 years ago.

The *I Ching* uses the hexagrams to help us resolve conflicting ideas. We may have doubts about the wisdom of starting a new venture, getting married or moving to a new location. The hexagrams confront us with a constellation of archetypal binary opposites – favorable/unfavorable, gain/loss, advancing/retreating. Using the binary logic of yes and no, pro and con, the *I Ching* holds up a mirror to confront us with ourselves. It wants to make us aware that the question we ask contains the seed of the answer. Marysol Sterling Gonzalez, who studied the *I Ching* in the context of transpersonal psychology, aptly referred to the book as a "psychological computer." She points out the I Ching does not give us a precise response to questions: rather, the book puts us in contact with our subconscious, which knows the answer.

We can be skeptical about the usefulness of the *I Ching* and still recognize that its fundamental (binary) principle shaped Chinese civilization. The *I Ching* dates from the Western Zhou period (1000–750 BCE). One of the earliest versions of the book is known as *Zhou Yi*. All other Chinese classics that shaped Chinese civilization are based on the *Zhou Yi*. China's ancient rulers consulted the book to "steer" the ship of state. Confucius famously said that if he had fifty more years to live, he would devote half of them studying the *I Ching*. The binary yin-yang logic of the *I Ching* formed the basis of nearly all Chinese disciplines.

16. Cybernetic logic

Gottfried Leibniz was only the first of many Western thinkers to be captivated by Chinese cosmogony. Danish physicist Niels Bohr used the yin-yang symbol for his family coat-of-arms, together with the motto 'contraria sunt complementa', (opposites are complementary). Carl Jung wrote a foreword to Wilhelm-Baynes' translation of the *I Ching* and Hermann Hesse's 1943 novel *The Glass Bead Game* is said to deal in part with the principles of the *I Ching*. Allen Ginsberg wrote a poem called 'Consulting I Ching Smoking Pot Listening to the Fugs Sing

Black', and Bob Dylan referred to the *I Ching* in his song 'Idiot Wind' (I threw the I Ching yesterday/it said there might be some thunder at the well). George Harrison opened the *I Ching* randomly, saw the words "gently weeps," and wrote the legendary song 'While My Guitar Gently Weeps'.

Yet the story of the *I Ching* and Leibniz has another dimension that takes us from ancient China to the modern science of cybernetics.

In 1956, the British Sinologist Joseph Needham published the second volume of his monumental study *Science and Civilization of China*. Needham describes Leibniz's encounter with China and pointed at the apparent correlation between the Chinese binary system and the modern science of cybernetics. Needham referred to the-then new computer science developed by the American scientist Norbert Wiener. Needham explained that Wiener, like most other computer scientists in the 1940s, had opted for the binary systems in computer design. Needham wrote: "It [the binary code] has been found to be, as Wiener points out in his important book on cybernetics (the study of self-regulating systems whether animal or mechanical), the most suitable system for the great computing machines of the present day. It has been found convenient to build them on a binary basis, using only 'on' and 'off' positions, whether of switches in electrical circuits or of thermonic valves, and the type of algorithm followed is therefore the Boolean algebra of classes, which gives only the choice of 'yes' or 'no', of being either inside a class or outside. It is therefore no coincidence that Leibniz, besides developing the binary arithmetic, was also the founder of modern mathematical logic and a pioneer in the construction of calculating machines. As we may see later, Chinese influence was responsible, at least in part, for his conception of an algebraic or mathematical logic, just as the system of order in the Book of Changes foreshadowed the binary arithmetic."

In the 1940s, Norbert Wiener was appointed as head of a team of scientists tasked by the US government to develop computing machines with unrivaled accuracy. The military needed high-speed calculations for breaking enemy codes, ballistic tables, anti-aircraft gun-sight predictor mechanisms and avionics for guided missile systems. Wiener assembled an interdisciplinary team that included neurophysiologists who had discovered that neurophysiological bodies are controlled by minuscule electrical impulses that alternate between on and off. Wiener and his team decided computing machines could mimic this binary principle, and opted for Leibniz's binary code to develop high-speed computers.

After the war, Wiener wrote his landmark book *Cybernetics: Or Control and Communication in the Animal and the Machine.* The subtitle refers to the fact that Wiener and his team applied the electrical on-off impulses in biological bodies to their computing machine. Wiener, who proposed Gottfried Leibniz as the Patron Saint of cybernetics, laid the groundwork for the first coherent computer science that could be applied to many other disciplines, among them engineering, systems control, cognitive systems, biology, neuroscience and even the organization of society. One of the most important technologies resulting from cybernetics is the automatic pilot, an indispensable instrument in modern aviation.

Cybernetics introduced two important new concepts: state and feedback. A cybernetic system like an autopilot in an airliner operates within a set of parameters set by the navigator. To assure the system remains within the set parameters, the autopilot takes constant readings of the actual state of the airliner (position, altitude, speed, etc.) against the parameters set by the navigator. Feedback from a compass, sensors, GPS and other instruments will show discrepancies between the actual state of the aircraft and the preprogrammed state – the difference between where it actually is and where it should be. If discrepancies are found, the autopilot will take corrective action based on Boolean logic: IF strong side winds push the aircraft off course, THEN the ailerons in the wings will effect a course correction. The cybernetic method can be summarized with three words: plan, quantify, and steer. The method can be applied to any conceivable human activity.

17. Intelligence and artificial intelligence

An autopilot in an airliner relies on a computer and is called a cybernetic system. A computer programmed designed to play chess or drive a car is called artificial intelligence. The former is designed to perform a specific task, that latter can be programmed to "self-learn." Based on current technology, the distinction is artificial; a cybernetic system can easily be designed for self-learning. Both cybernetics and AI rely on

Boolean logic, an endless sequence of IF/THEN – if A is true, B is false. Artificial intelligence could have been called Second Generation Cybernetics – less intriguing, but it would have avoided the argument of what constitutes intelligence and the fear of unintended consequences. Some AI scientists predict AI will ultimately lead to the development robots that can take over the world and render humans superfluous.

For now, AI is constrained by the same parameters as cybernetics. Both AI and cybernetics rely on logic and intention. The binary/Boolean logic is universal, the intention is determined by the designer of the system. A navigator for an aircraft programs the autopilot by selecting a destination from the available options. An autopilot cannot be programmed to fly to an imaginary airport. A computer designed to play chess is based on the same logic, but has a different intention: winning. IBM's Big Blue relied on Boolean logic to beat a world champion simply by processing probabilities: "IF white moves D4, THEN black will counter with C5." Beating a world champion is impressive, but it is not magic. A computer powerful enough and using efficient algorithms can simply weigh and process more options faster than humans can. If a chess computer makes an occasional move not anticipated by its programmers, it still operates within the confines of binary/Boolean logic.

AI designed for any other task operates on the basis of the same principles. A self-driving vehicle is equipped with cameras and other sensors to read its environment and designed to respond in real-time, just like an autopilot. A computer programmer will model the required functions in computer code "analogous" to reality - roads, traffic signs, vehicles, railroad crossings and all other aspect of the traffic environment. The vehicle responds to its environment using Boolean logic: IF the on-board camera detects a red traffic light, THEN the car will apply the brakes and stop. IF it hears the siren of a fire truck while approaching a green traffic light at an intersection, THEN it will stop and give way. AI systems are "multi-sensory" versions of so-called expert systems.

18. Analog or digital, that's the question

The more ominous claims made by AI experts are based on the assumption that unlimited computing power will allow us to "reverse-engineer" the human brain or decode its content and save it as a backup copy to be reused or to "upgrade" a brain suffering from Alzheimer. It presumably would capture human consciousness developed from birth, the acquisition of concepts and values, development of emotional bonds, urge to procreate, dormant memories activated by sounds of smells, response to fear and hope and an awareness of mortality. Apart from the complexities of understanding or reverse-engineering the human brain, digital technology will have to take into account that human faculties like hearing, seeing, feeling, and body language are "analog" and, for now, must be modeled in binary code.

In the 1950s, binary computers replaced most analog computers. The former proved to be more stable, and simplified computation using Boolean logic. This would lead to the digital revolution impacting the world starting in the 1970s. However, digital systems merely translate analog products. "Digital music" doesn't exist. A digital recording stores binary numbers obtained by "sampling" or quantizing an analog audio wave thousands of times a second in discrete segments. Each "sample" is given a binary number, which is converted back into an audible (analog) sound wave by a digital-analog converter. The high sampling rate of the audio wave obscures the fact that it has been digitized in discrete steps, even tough audiophiles claim to hear the difference between digitized and analog recordings. Most people take the "missing" information between the sampled audio for granted.

The analog-digital question was addressed by American neurophysiologist Ralph Gerard at the legendary Macy Conferences held between 1946 and 1953. The conferences brought together a diverse, interdisciplinary community of scholars and researchers to lay the groundwork for the new science of cybernetics, and "to restore unity to science." Gerard took issue with the consensus view at the conference that the brain was comparable to a calculation machine. Gerard said: "To take what is learned from working with calculating machines and communication systems, and to explore the use of these insights in interpreting the action of the brain, is admirable; but to say, as the public press says, that therefore these machines are brains, and that our brains are nothing but calculating machines, is presumptuous." Ralph Gerald noted that the electrical activity in the nervous system is analog while the nerve impulse appears to be digital. Science historian

George Dyson and physicist Freeman Dyson insisted the brain itself is an analog computer, while biologists think of DNA as digital.

19. Aesthetic view

Quantum physics theorists confronted with the wave-particle duality have their own issues with the analog-digital dichotomy. They point out the wave is analog while the particle is digital. Newtonian mechanics and Maxwell's electromagnetic field equations are considered analog and particle physics is digital. Modern physics generally assumed the world follows the rules of quantum mechanics. Scholars in other domains have offered their own view. British anthropologist Gregory Bateson argued that written and spoken language is digital because of the arbitrary assignment of words to their meanings, while paralinguistics (body language, gestures, facial expressions) are analogical.

Cameron McEwen, in his essay 'The Digital Wittgenstein', shows that Ludwig Wittgenstein, influential 20th century Austrian-British philosopher of logic and language, was one of many other thinkers who addressed the nature of the analog-digital. McEwen mentioned thinkers like Samuel Beckett, Martin Heidegger,

Soren Kierkegaard, Immanuel Kant, (perhaps inspired by Leibniz), going all the way back to Plato. McEwen wrote: "It is an unfailing mark of the greatest thinkers of the tradition, like Plato, that they recognize the digital possibility and therefore recognize the principal difference of it from analog possibilities. From an analog position, by contrast, the digital possibility either does not exist at all or exists only in secondary fashion which is, therefore, deficient and demanding of analysis."

In recent years computer scientists have studied the possibility of integrating analog and digital on a single chip to better deal with dynamic and continuous systems like neural networks and for robots responding in real time, but the 'epistemological' debate will probably continue. In the realm of physics, we can compare analog and digital with force and equilibrium, dynamic and static. They are mutually dependent: force must be restrained by equilibrium and equilibrium requires force to remain a dynamic vitality. In the realm of aesthetics, we may conclude Europe had an analog perception of reality traceable to Greece, while China had a binary view of reality traceable to Tao. European architecture was analogous to the human form and European painting analogous to optical perception. Chinese architecture was based on the "binary" yin-yang principle of Tao, and its classic painting (invariably black and white, denoting yin and yang) was concerned with the underlying principle of nature rather than its outward appearance.

The two different views are best illustrated when we compare the Dutch master Rembrandt and the Chinese (Zen) master Muqi, and the Sacré-Cœur in Paris and Katsura Palace in Kyoto. They both reflect traditions going back more than 2000 years. Perception is what American media scholar Carol Wilders addressed when she wrote the paper 'Being Digital'. Wilder conducted an informal survey asking people what comes to mind when they think of analog and digital. Among the responses were body/mind, atoms/bits, pathos/logos, fax/email, Harley/Kawasaki, rolodex/database, gears/switches, qualitative/quantitative, hand/fingers, context/code, Later Wittgenstein/Early Wittgenstein, actual/virtual. The notions of analog and digital are, of course, human constructs and without independent existence. But they had an impact on the formation of culture in the past, and will no doubt have an impact on the future.

20. Road to Nirvana

Up to the 19th century China and Japan lived firmly in the Confucian "architectural grid" first developed in ancient China. The Qing dynasty in China (1644-1912) and the Edo period in Japan (1603-1868) remained largely unchanged for 300 years, without substantial progress in either science or art.

After World War II, barely within a generation, East Asia became the factory of the world, the leading producer of everything from electronics and appliances to motor vehicles, communications equipment and solar technology while using widely different political ideologies, which suggests they see ideology as a means to an end, not the Holy Grail of modernity. In the 1980s, when Japan had regained its confidence, prominent industrial designer Kenji Ekuan gave his view of our current age. "The world has seen great dramas in the past," he said. "We have seen the French Revolution, the American Revolution, the Russian Revolution. But now the world is awaiting a new drama. I call it the drama of the material world."

China's economic miracle is repeating the Japanese success on a much larger scale. The country provided basic human needs like housing, food, education and electricity to more than half of its 1.4 billion people, while becoming an economic and technological superpower. It launched infrastructure projects like the new Silk Road (One Belt, One Road) to link the vast Eurasian, including Western Asia and the Indian subcontinent.

India has historically viewed China as a rival, if not an existential threat. But India has been influenced by China via the West. All Indian architects building today's homes, factories and offices are, unwittingly, using Chinese axonometry and most advanced products and equipment used in India have components made in China. When India builds factories, Chinese factories are the benchmark and when India designs its own version of the Internet of Things (IoT), it will rely primarily on Chinese hardware and much of the AI-software.

China will become the leading Internet nation and dominant in the IoT, which will imbue virtually the entire "material world" with Internet-based artificial intelligence. The influence that comes from being the world's largest manufacturer and having data on billions of people from all over the world can only be imagined. China is developing AI systems for every conceivable human domain: education, medical treatment planning, ecological management, business strategy, cyber security, physical security, finance and traffic management systems for self-driving vehicles in the largest road system in the world. Producing both the hardware and software for a technological society equipped with the IoT connected to AI systems will enable China to set global standards.

Like the Japanese, the Chinese are not overly concerned about robots taking over the world, replacing human beings, or AI outsmarting humans, as some Western AI experts predict. East Asians are pragmatic. A Japanese entrepreneur, asked on American television if he feared AI would lead to war, could barely hold back a chuckle before saying that truly intelligent AI will know war is not an economic way to resolve conflict. A Chinese entrepreneur asked if robots could control humans in the future argued that machine intelligence comes from the brain, but wisdom and love come from the heart. They seem unconcerned about evil minds donating their intelligence to AI. For now, AI is the adolescent younger brother of cybernetics. Unless instructed by the designer to do otherwise, AI will not make up non-existing facts, just like an autopilot will not fly an aircraft to a non-existing airport. In both sciences, intention is the key. History explains why the Chinese, like the Japanese, have no fear of technology. Reconciling robots and humans is simply the modern equivalent of the age-old practice of reconciling spirit and matter.

* * *